the guide to owning a
Dove

Nikki Moustaki

T.F.H. Publications, Inc.
One TFH Plaza
Third and Union Avenues
Neptune City, NJ 07753

This book has been published with the intent to provide accurate and authoritative information in regard to the subject matter within. While every precaution has been taken in preparation of this book, the publisher and author assume no responsibility for errors or omissions. Neither is any liability assumed for damages resulting from the use of the information herein.

Library of Congress Cataloging-in-Publication Data
Moustaki, Nikki, 1970-
The guide to owning a dove / Nikki Moustaki.
p. cm.
ISBN 0-7938-2216-5 (alk. paper)
1.Pigeons. I. Title.
SF465.M68 2004
598.6'5--dc22
2003022006

www.tfh.com

Contents

Doves have been symbols of peace and serenity since ancient times. Today, many people are turning to doves as companion pets. (Ivory-white Silky Ringneck, male)

THE GUIDE TO OWNING A DOVE

Introducing the Dove

The dove has long been a symbol of peace and freedom, viewed worldwide as a messenger of serenity and safety. It is the mascot for many organizations and is an animal of Biblical notoriety. The dove exists in

The Ringneck dove, also called the Barbary Dove, is one of the most commonly kept birds in the dove family. (Tangerine Ringneck)

every country and on every continent, with the exception of Antarctica. Images of doves are seen in very early artifacts, indicating that humans have had a relationship with them for a very long time. Many people turn to doves as companion pets, and those who live with doves soon discover that they are enchanting and charming additions to the home, not just beautiful icons.

The dove is a "smaller" version of the animal we call the pigeon, though some species of doves are actually larger than the average feral street pigeon. Both the pigeon and the dove are found in the same scientific order, Columbiformes, and in the same family, Columbidae. For the purposes of this book, we'll consider doves to be the more diminutive, finer species of pigeon. Most of the information in this book can be used to care for pigeons as well, but this book will focus on doves specifically, treating them as separate animals from pigeons.

Doves are found in the same scientific order, Columbiformes, and family, Columbidae, as pigeons. (Pied Ringneck, three weeks old)

Doves are typically split into two categories: seed-eaters and fruit-eaters. The fruit-eaters are not usually kept in the average home but can be found in zoos or in the aviaries of serious hobbyists. It's likely that you'll be starting with the more commonly kept seed-eating species. More advanced dove keepers also stick with the seed-eating varieties of doves and turn their attentions to breeding and mutations (color varieties).

Most doves are relatively muted in color, especially if you compare them to parrots and other exotic birds, but some of the commonly kept doves, such as the Ringneck and the Diamond Dove, have various color mutations that are quite exciting to the avid dovekeeper. Some fruit doves, however, can be quite colorful and striking.

Aside from color differences, most doves look relatively the same anatomically. They have large bodies in proportion to the head and a pointed beak that dips downward slightly at the tip.

Like most birds, doves can detect moving objects better than humans, a function of the prey/predator relationship. Doves have to be able to quickly see a predator so that they can fly away before being caught. Doves also have a third eyelid underneath the exterior eyelids that helps keep the eye healthy by brushing away debris.

Doves' ears are located parallel to their eyes and are covered by feathers. Most doves can hear low-frequen-

An outdoor garden setting is the perfect place to house doves in a temperate climate. (Cream Pied Ringneck)

cy sounds at incredible distances. They don't seem to hear at the very upper and lower ends of the frequency scale, but what they hear in the middle of the range is similar to what humans hear.

The beak is made of the same material as human fingernails. It grows over a honeycomb-like structure and is light enough to allow the bird to fly. The beak is part of the dove's complex digestive system. After food is swallowed it goes to the crop, a sac-like organ near the dove's breast. After being softened in the crop, the food goes to the stomach (proventriculus), then on to the gizzard (ventriculus), which grinds the food with

the help of *grit*. Grit is available to birds in the form of sand (indigestible grit), ground eggshells, oyster shells, and other forms of digestible grit sold in pet shops. Doves eat small amounts of grit as they feed each day. Food that is not absorbed into the bird's system moves on to the cloaca, the place where waste collects before being eliminated by way of the vent. The nostrils (nares) are just above the beak.

Doves use their feet to help regulate body temperature—when his environment is cold, a dove can decrease the amount of blood circulating to his legs, and will often draw one leg up

Most of the commonly kept doves are ground dwellers. (Pink Ringneck)

into his body and stand on one leg. He will also keep his feathers fluffed and extended from his body to keep warm air close to his skin. When a dove is warm, he can increase the blood flow to his legs to cool off.

Doves and pigeons are extraordinary athletes, able to fly for miles a day—one pigeon was clocked at flying for 600 miles at a stretch. Your dove's bones are light, thin-walled, and are filled with air, all necessary aspects for flight.

Many of the commonly kept doves spend a lot of time on the ground pecking around for food or going though mating rituals. Other doves are primarily tree dwellers, and some split their time between the ground and a higher perch. If you have a mixed aviary planned, it's a good idea to combine these birds rather than combining two ground-dwelling species or two tree-dwelling species—this way the two won't compete as much for space or food.

TYPES OF DOVES

There are more than 300 species of doves/pigeons, but the average bird keeper does not keep many of these species. Below is a list of five types of doves common to the pet trade and suitable for beginners. There are, of course, many others, but these are great to start with. You can always move on to more challenging doves when you're successful with these:

There are more than 300 species of doves and pigeons, but only a few dozen are readily available in the pet trade. (Ringneck)

The Ringneck or Barbary Dove
(Streptopelia risoria)

This hardy bird, bred and domesticated from an African species, is one of the most commonly kept doves. They don't have extreme housing requirements and are quite easy to breed. As of this writing, the Ringneck Dove comes in more than 40 color mutations. This dove is in the turtle-dove family because, like the others in this group, it has a ring around its neck. This bird can be found in most pet shops, and plenty of hobbyists breed, sell, and trade them.

The Diamond Dove
(Geopelia cuneata)

This Australian native is one of the smallest, most popular doves and comes in more than a dozen color mutations. It is not the easiest dove to breed and may be intimidated by larger species in an aviary. Easily found in most pet shops and bred by many hobbyists, the Diamond Dove requires a smaller seed mix than other doves—finch and canary mix will do.

The Mourning Dove
(Zenaida macroura)

Named for its melancholic coo, the Mourning Dove is also known as the Wood Dove and Grayson's Dove. This dove, which is native to North and South America, is relatively easy to keep and breed and is peaceful in an aviary setting.

The Laceneck Dove
(Streptopelia chinensis)

This hardy dove, also called the Chinese Turtle Dove and the Spotted Turtle Dove, is peaceful with other doves unless it's crowded during mating and nesting.

The Rock Dove
(Columba livia)

This is the common feral pigeon—a great bird for beginners. Rock doves are very hardy and easy to keep in all climates, come in a wide variety of mutations, and are "free-breeders"—they breed readily. Because Rock Doves have homing instincts, you can let them leave the coop in the morning and know that they will return in the evening.

Whichever kind of dove you decide to keep, you will probably want to join a dove club in your area or a dove mailing list on the Internet that will put you in touch with bird keepers all over the world. Don't be afraid to ask dove hobbyists a lot of questions—they generally love to share what they've learned.

Meanwhile, this book offers basic information that anyone starting out in doves needs to know. It will help you decide which types of doves are right for you, prepare to bring them home, house them properly, feed them well, help them when they're ill, and breed them, should you choose to do that.

Selecting and Safekeeping Your Dove

Doves are relatively easy to care for and don't need the kind of hands-on attention that many other birds need. Doves can be hand-tamed, however, and they make friendly companions. They are great for children because they don't bite (though their nails can get sharp if left untrimmed), and they aren't loud, the way some parrots are. However, please note that only responsible children should be allowed to have doves as pets.

When you bring *any* pet into your home, it's important to consider whether you have the time to properly care for it, the money to take it to a veterinarian should it become ill, and the willingness to do whatever it takes to give the animal a bountiful and happy life. Someone in the home should truly love the animal.

COMMITMENT

Though doves are easily cared for, they require a time commitment, just as any pet does. They must be fed and watered daily and watched for signs of illness. Daily cleaning of the aviary or cage is absolutely necessary, as is weekly maintenance, cleaning, and disinfecting. Yearly vaccinations may be necessary as well. Ill doves absolutely must have access to veterinary care. Remember that most doves can live to be between 10 and 30 years of age if properly cared for, so this isn't a relationship to be entered into lightly.

Besides time, you also have to commit enough space for your doves, either inside your home or outside, in an aviary or flight cage. Keeping doves outside will add another responsibility—watching the weather and maintaining your birds' housing accordingly.

This pet Ringneck is tame enough to have some free time outside of the cage. (Ringneck)

MAINTENANCE

Even though doves do not require the hands-on time that other birds do, they do require specific attention to keep them healthy. The following is a list of dove maintenance tasks.

Daily

- Rotate all food and water dishes with clean, disinfected dishes.
- Offer clean, dry seed.
- Offer fresh water.
- Clean the bottom of the cage (if keeping the doves in a cage).
- Hose down the aviary's concrete floor (if keeping the doves in an aviary).
- Make sure each bird is behaving normally.

Weekly

- Scrape perches clean.
- Sanitize the bottom of the aviary or cage.
- Rake the dirt or sand on the aviary floor.

Monthly

- Sanitize the entire cage or aviary with a 10-percent bleach solution and rinse thoroughly.
- Turn the aviary's dirt or sand floor.

Yearly

- Replace the aviary's dirt or sand floor (as needed).
- Provide vaccinations (where applicable).
- If your doves breed, clean the nesting sites thoroughly.

CHOOSING DOVES

Only buy doves that are exhibited in a clean environment. They should have enough food and water and not be crowded together. You can't be sure that a dove you buy on the spot is free of disease, but he's more likely to be infected with something if the birds are living in cramped squalor.

You want the dove you select to be healthy. Look for an active dove with sleek, tight feathers, a clean beak, clear eyes and nares (nostrils), and clean, intact feet. Feel the dove's keel bone (breastbone) to make sure he's not too thin, an indicator of possible disease. The bird should be meaty on either side of the keel bone. Stools should be well formed, not watery.

Stay away from any dove that has the following symptoms, which may indicate illness: swollen, cloudy eyes; any discharge from the eyes, nose, mouth, or vent; tail bobbing; a fluffed-up appearance; listlessness; loss of appetite; lameness; panting or labored breathing; or debris around the face or on the feathers.

Keeping More Than One Dove

Many experts advocate keeping doves in pairs, and most people keep doves in a male/female pair. Doves in a mixed pair are often more contented than lone doves or doves living with same-sex birds only. However, it's not easy to tell the difference between the sexes, and even the most experienced bird keepers can err when trying to determine the sex of young birds.

Some breeders may agree to swap birds with you if you have bought a same-sex pair, or you can try again and buy two more birds to pair up with your original pair.

If you want to own more than one dove, try to buy them all at the same time, so you can put them in their cage or aviary at the same time. If you let some birds become established and then add other birds, the birds that were already there may harass and even kill the new birds. Make sure the pair (or pairs) that you buy is a true, mixed pair—a male and a female. If

A fluffed-up appearance doesn't always indicate illness—the bird could simply feel a bit chilled or cold. (Tangerine Pearl Ringneck, female)

Try to obtain a "true pair"—a male and female—from the start.

you buy a batch of young, unpaired birds, you'll have to wait to see how (and if) they pair up, and there are no guarantees you'll have the proper mix of males and females. This is not a crisis, because if you have more of one gender than the other, you can always trade off with another dove hobbyist.

It's advisable to be careful about keeping your doves with other birds. Some doves can be kept with finches or canaries, but watch for aggression. Even a little finch can become aggressive toward a larger dove and try to pull out his feathers or terrorize his nesting site.

BRINGING HOME A NEW DOVE
Quarantine new doves from your other birds for at least 30 days to make certain the new bird isn't carrying a contagious disease or parasites. If you tend to the new bird before the bird or birds you already have,

make sure to change your clothes and wash your hands thoroughly when you leave the new bird and before you approach the established birds. Take the newcomer to your avian veterinarian if you notice anything wrong with him.

Give your new dove a chance to get used to his new home before you try to tame him or place him in a large aviary. Doves are sensitive and can panic in a new environment. Put the dove in his new cage or a temporary cage and leave him alone except for feeding, watering, and cleaning for at least ten days. Once the bird eats well and becomes active, you can begin to include him in your everyday life and allow him around your other birds.

DOVE-PROOFING YOUR HOME
Before you bring your doves home, you should make sure that your home is safe for them. Many common household objects can be extremely dangerous for your doves, so you must "dove-proof" your home so that these dangers can be avoided. The following section covers the most common dangers that take the lives of pet doves. Keeping a close eye on the whereabouts of your bird at all times can also help your bird avoid any potential dangers.

Standing Water
Doves are attracted to water and can drown easily by falling into deep water while trying to bathe or drink.

Most doves aren't allowed to fly around the house, but plenty of them are, and doves that are allowed more freedom in a home where they're not being supervised closely can easily find water and potentially drown. Doves that are allowed to fly in the house can also run into other dangers, such as flying into a mirror or closed window, flying out of a window, or flying onto a hot stove.

Toilet Bowls

Close all toilet lids, even if you think your bird can't get to the bathroom and especially if he can.

Pools and Jacuzzis

If your bird has access to these, keep a close eye on him when he's out of the cage. Fountains and ponds hold the same danger.

Dog Bowls

If you have a dog that has a large dog dish, your dove might find his way into the center of it and not be able to get out.

Fish Tanks and Fish Bowls

A dove might want to bathe in them, so make sure to protect your pet from this potential hazard.

Drinking Glasses

A half-empty drinking glass may entice a dove to drink, and he may fall in and be unable to get out.

Standing Water in the Kitchen

Full sinks and pots boiling on the stove pose grave dangers for your birds. Keep an eye on the sink when you're soaking dishes and keep all cooking pots tightly covered. The same goes for your large appliances,

Keeping your dove in a safe environment is essential—this dove is properly housed and can find shelter if needed. (Light Ash Ringneck)

such as the dishwasher and washing machine—your dove could fly in unnoticed and you might turn on the machine.

Predators

You absolutely must keep your dove away from your other pets. Even when cats and dogs are very well fed, they may still be tempted to prey on your doves. Cats and most dogs like to chase small, quick-moving animals.

Even a brief encounter with a cat or dog can be deadly. Cats have a type of bacteria on their nails and in their mouths, and even the slightest cut can cause infection and death in your bird in as few as 48 hours. A dog can frighten a bird to death just by playing with him. Also, there may be injuries that you don't see after a run-in with the family cat or dog. If contact does occur, take your bird to your avian veterinarian immediately.

Additionally, other pets, such as snakes, ferrets, and rats will not think twice about eating or injuring your dove. Snakes also are notorious for sneaking into cages.

Your immediate response to any animal bite should be to call your avian veterinarian or any available veterinarian immediately. You can flush a small wound with a weak solution of hydrogen peroxide and water before you leave the house for the veterinarian's office. If the wound is large, leave it

Keep all doves away from other pets that can harm them, especially cats, dogs, ferrets, rats, and snakes. (Tangerine Ringneck)

Doves housed outside won't have to contend with indoor dangers, though they are susceptible to harsh weather conditions and predators. (Roan Ringneck, female)

alone and rush your bird to the veterinarian.

Nonstick Cookware and Appliances

Heated, nonstick cookware emits a colorless, odorless fume that kills birds immediately. It was previously thought that only nonstick cookware that was burned or overheated emitted fumes, but there have been cases where birds have died from normal cooking temperatures. Birds have also died from self-cleaning ovens during the cleaning process.

Nonstick surfaces can be found in just about any kitchen appliance or cooking utensil that you can think of and that is designated "nonstick," including the following: stovetop burners, drip pans for burners, broiler pans, griddles, woks, waffle makers, electric skillets, deep fryers, crock pots, popcorn poppers, coffee makers, bread makers, non-stick rolling pins, candy molds, stockpots, roasters, and pizza pans. Nonstick surfaces are not restricted to cooking tools. They are also found in such household items as irons, portable heaters, heat lamps, and ironing board covers.

Obviously, dove owners still need to be able to cook and may still want to use some of the appliances listed here.

The solution is to *never* buy cookware or appliances that are designated "nonstick" and to make sure that the appliances and cookware you do own are *not* nonstick. Make sure all of your kitchenware is safe for your bird—and, as an added precaution, make sure your bird never goes near the kitchen while your cooking.

Other Common Household Products

Products that you regularly use in your home can be deadly to your dove. These products include cleansers and candles, items you wouldn't think of as poisonous. There aren't many commercial cleansers that aren't harmful to birds if ingested or applied on the skin. When cleaning your bird's cage, rinse it thoroughly before placing the bird back inside—or, you can opt to use safer cleansers, such as baking soda as an abrasive cleanser and vinegar as a disinfectant—these things will not harm your bird the way a detergent can.

Common household products that you should keep far away from your bird include:

- Barbecue items, such as charcoal and lighter fluid;
- Cleansers, soaps, and detergents;
- Scented products, such as scented candles, candle "beads," and air fresheners;
- Insecticides, such as rodent poisons, roach and rodent traps;
- Crayons, markers, pens, and pencils;
- Plant fertilizers.

Houseplants

Your dove may nibble on your houseplants, and some of them can be deadly. You may also want to plant vegetation in your aviary, and you should make sure that you use only safe foliage. Fresh trees and tree branches are wonderful additions to a dove's environment, but only if they are free of pesticides and fertilizers. Wash all plants and tree parts thoroughly before placing them near your bird.

Safe indoor plants include the following:

Acacia Aloe, African Violet, Baby's Tears, Bamboo, Begonia, Bougainvillea, Chickweed, Christmas Cactus, Cissus/Kangaroo Vine, Coffee, Coleus, Crabapple, Dandelion, Dogwood, Ferns, Figs, Gardenia, Herbs, Jade Plant, Marigold, Nasturtium, Petunia, Prayer Plant, Purple Passion/Velvet, Spider Plant, Swedish Ivy, Thistle, White Clover, and Zebra Plant.

Outdoor plants that are safe to include in your cage or aviary include the following: Apple, Arbutus, Ash, Aspen, Beech, Birch, Citrus (any), Cottonwood, Dogwood, Elm, Eucalyptus, Fir, Guava, Hawthorn, Larch, Magnolia, Manzanita, Norfolk Island Pine, Palms, Pear, Pine, Poplar, Willow, and Sequoia (Redwood).

Open Windows and Doors

Be very careful about open windows and doors if you let your dove have free run of your home, even for a few

To ensure your pet's safety, keep all doves away from common household products and be very careful of open windows. (Fantail dove)

hours a day. Keep screens on your windows and make sure your bird is in his cage when you open the door. Some pigeons have homing instincts and return home if they fly away, but most doves don't. Some people who keep their doves indoors prevent fly-aways and indoor accidents by clipping the their doves' wings, a painless grooming method meant to protect a bird's safety.

Ceiling Fans

Doves instinctually fly to the highest point, and this is often the ceiling fan. A ceiling fan that's turned on and a bird that's flying around the room are a deadly combination. Make sure that your ceiling fan is off when your bird is out of his cage.

Toxic Foods

Most foods are fine to share with your dove, but some can be deadly or, at the very least, make him ill. Never share alcohol, chocolate, avocado, raw onions, or raw rhubarb with your bird.

Feet and Doors

Many birds have been killed in slamming doors or under a big sneaker. Such accidents are more likely to happen if your bird is nearly the same color as your floor.

Lead and Other Metals

Stained glass, chipping paint, jewelry parts, lead weights, and fishing lures can contain lead, and your curious dove may want to see what these things taste like. Metal poisoning is difficult to treat and causes an agonizing death. Keep all metal objects away from your bird.

Mirrors, Glass, and Walls

A bird that has not had his wings clipped is often in danger of flying headlong into things. Birds may mistake what they see in squeaky-clean window glass and mirrors for flight paths, and young birds that aren't skilled flyers might bump into walls and furnishings. If you opt not to clip your bird's wings to prevent such mishaps, keep your windows and mirrors dirty, purchase stickers for them, or hang an attractive plastic window decoration (not stained glass). You also might consider not giving your young bird full flight in the house until he understands his flying abilities.

Temperature Extremes

Doves can stand a wide temperature range, say between 32°F and 90°F (depending on the species), but they are prone to chill, frostbite, and overheating when the temperature goes to an extreme beyond the comfort range. Avoid this by making sure that your dove lives in a controlled environment where the temperature is constant—between 70°F and 80°F is very comfortable for a dove. Fluctuations in temperature, like those found in kitchens or bathrooms, should be avoided on a long-term basis.

Housing Your Dove

There are several ways to house doves, but most dove keepers will agree that the larger the housing, the better. Though many people keep smaller doves like Diamonds and Ringnecks indoors, doves need a large space where they can fly and live peaceably together. Remember that many doves will spend a good deal of time on the aviary floor, and a small

Many people keep Ringneck Doves inside, but these doves do appreciate a larger space where they can fly, such as an aviary. (Ringneck)

Most doves can live peaceably in groups if given enough room. Never crowd your doves. (Ringnecks)

cage just doesn't allow this natural behavior. An aviary is ideal because it's large and allows the doves to behave naturally and get enough exercise. Some doves can be kept in a cage inside the house and allowed free roam of the house or a certain room when they can be supervised. Very tame doves have been known to be wonderful pets when kept this way.

HOUSING SIZE

Unlike parrots and other birds, doves don't climb around the cage, so they need room to fly. House your doves in the largest cage that your budget and space can afford. If you can't provide a large space (or some free-flying time inside your home), your doves won't be very happy, and they certainly won't be very healthy.

When considering housing size, always plan for pairs, because it's likely that you won't have just one dove, even if that's your initial intention. Depending on their size, each pair will need a certain amount of cubic footage in a cage or aviary. Remember that height matters less than length and width, because doves fly back and forth, not up and down. The cage should be at least 2 to 4 feet high, but it can be as high as you'd like.

For pairs of smaller doves, the smallest ideal cage is 3x3x3 feet, though I recommend something much bigger. For the larger doves and pigeons, consider a cage that is at least 3x6 feet or 4x5 feet per pair, though some of the largest species will need more space than that.

If you want to keep your doves in an aviary, base the size of the enclosure on how many doves you want to keep or breed. If you have already acquired an aviary, base the number of doves it could contain on its cubic footage. Small doves require a minimum of 27 cubic feet per dove, and the larger doves and pigeons should have at least 50 to 60 cubic feet. If you decide to keep pigeons with your doves, also remember that pigeons are more aggressive and will need more space. Keep in mind that cubic feet are measured by multiplying width by height by length. Calculate the cubic feet of your aviary, then divide by 27 (or by 60 for pigeons or larger doves), and you'll come up with the number of birds that your aviary can sustain healthily.

For example, an aviary that is 10 feet wide, 7 feet high, and 5 feet long has 350 cubic feet. Divide that by 27, and you come up with approximately 12 birds, or 6 pairs, the maximum number of small doves your aviary can sustain peaceably. If you have larger doves or pigeons, divide by 60 to come up with approximately 6 birds, or 3 pairs, for this particular aviary.

AVOIDING AGGRESSION

When planning how many doves you want to keep and where you want to keep them, remember that cramping your doves in too small a space is not only unhealthy, it can make aggressive species fight among each other and pester more docile species. Males are more likely to squabble anyway, but the more space you give them, the less violent the squabbling will be.

Another good way to avoid aggression in the aviary is to mix species so that you eliminate competition for food. One half of your doves can be ground-dwellers, while the rest can be tree-dwellers. You can also make sure that each species is from a different ecological region. Doves from regions that overlap will instinctively compete for food and territory.

Remember that each large dove needs at least 50 cubic feet of space in an aviary—crowding can cause fighting and illness. (Tangerine Silky Ringneck, male)

You can keep your doves in cages or aviaries, outside or inside. Let's look at the options.

THE WALK-IN AVIARY

The Frame

The best space for doves is a walk-in aviary along one side of your home or another structure. The solid wall gives the aviary a secure starting point, as well as some protection from nasty weather. The structure should have a solid shelter on one end and a flight space on the other.

If you're handy, it's as easy as building a frame from untreated wood or concrete blocks and covering it with heavy-gauge wire. You can also use hardware cloth, a stiff but flexible metal mesh that has one-half-inch holes, which prevent predators from getting at your stock. Because the cloth is galvanized (treated with zinc),

you need to weather it before use. Liberally spray the roll with a solution of 50-percent white vinegar and 50-percent water. Then, unravel the roll, scrub it with a stiff scrub brush, and rinse it. Leave the roll outside for a couple of weeks (or more) in the rain and sun. By the time you build your aviary, the wire should be weathered enough so that it won't pose a danger to your doves.

The Shelter

You can construct a simple shelter by attaching corrugated fiberglass to one-third of the top of the cage and one-third of the sides, or you can be as elaborate as your imagination will allow. I've seen people use covered gazebos, pre-built wooden sheds, and intricately home-built shelters. I've even seen people use their patio or a room in their home as the shelter, adding an outside flight through a window.

This male Cape Dove may be small, but he won't like cramped housing. Consider an aviary when housing your doves. (Cape)

THE GUIDE TO OWNING A DOVE

Tree limbs and branches make great perches, but make sure they are free from pesticides, fungicides, and other chemicals before you use them. (Tangerine Ringneck)

Perches and Shelves

Place most of your perches in the shelter area, allowing a lot of free space in the flight for uninterrupted flying. Perches should be of various sizes and diameters. Natural perches are great because they promote good foot health. Make sure not to place perches over feeding and watering stations or above each other.

Live trees are great in the flight area as long as they're nontoxic, don't have thorns or other sharp growths, are spacious enough to allow perching, and don't crowd the whole flight area. The shelter should also have flat surfaces for roosting. Shelves of about 6 to 8 inches wide are fine for roosting. Make sure to clean these shelves when you make your daily rounds of the aviary. A spackle knife is perfect for scraping off dried droppings.

Flooring

Flooring for your aviary should be either concrete, natural dirt, or clean sand that you can buy from a toy store (for children's sandboxes). All have their advantages and disadvantages. A sloping concrete floor leading to a drain or other area where you can hose out the mess is great and easy to keep clean, as long as you have the time to clean it. It also allows you to inspect droppings and thoroughly disinfect the floor with a 10-percent bleach solution and a scrub brush.

Sand can be raked and provides grit, but it needs to be replaced a few times a year, depending on how many doves you have and how soiled it

Because doves are no match for outdoor predators, make sure you double-wire any outdoor cages. (Cape)

becomes. Both sand and natural dirt must have adequate drainage. If you choose the concrete floor, you can provide your doves with a pan of sand or dirt where they can scratch around.

Your doves will spend most of their day on the aviary floor, so some nice plantings or potted plants will give a more natural look and feel to the enclosure. Plants also offer some protection from males who tend to get aggressive when they want to breed.

Protection from Predators

Predators may try to get inside the aviary to consume your doves. Unless you have a concrete floor, you should line the entire floor with wire and cover it with soil or sand. Next, it's important to double-wire the cage so that determined predators won't be able to get to the birds. Place anoth-er layer of wire on top of the initial layer, making sure that there's at least an inch or more of space between the two layers. This is especially important to do on the bottom of suspended cages (which we'll get to in a moment).

The Double Door—An Aviary Must

A double door is a great idea for an aviary—in fact, you're likely to lose your doves without one, and doves are nearly impossible to catch once they've taken off. The double door allows you to enter the aviary without losing any of your birds to the open sky. Basically, you'll build a small enclosure, with its own door—like a small entrance vestibule—in front of the aviary door. When you walk into the vestibule from the outside, you'll close the vestibule door, then open the door to the aviary and walk into the aviary. If a dove does fly out of the aviary door, he can go no farther than the small enclosure.

Building a small enclosure inside the aviary will look more streamlined, but it takes space away from the inside of the aviary. You can even build a portable enclosure with three sides and wheels on the bottom so that you can move it from aviary to aviary, should you have more than one. Lock all doors with a quick link or a simple latch—I don't recommend using a padlock because you may need to enter the aviary quickly in an emergency. It's unlikely that someone will steal your doves, though it does happen, so find some other way to keep them safe, such as securing your yard and home.

Safety Padding

When doves become frightened, they fly upward, often pretty quickly, and can injure themselves on the top of the aviary and even die from the impact. Easily washable padding (such as the types used for insulation) or netting placed on or near the aviary's ceiling will prevent injury. Whether or not you do this really depends on the temperament of your individual doves.

Aviary Aesthetics

Finally, consider the aesthetics of the aviary. You can use non-toxic paint or stain to make the aviary match your home. Many people paint the inside of the aviary a light color so that the birds are easier to see. If you find that the hardware cloth or wire is too shiny and doesn't allow you to see your birds well, you can paint it darker with a non-toxic paint typically used for metal.

THE SUPPORTED OR SUSPENDED OUTSIDE CAGE

The suspended or supported outside cage is an alternative to the walk-in aviary. The cage is supported by sturdy legs or suspended from a structure by chains on each corner. Sturdy, wire mesh for this kind of cage is great, as is hardware cloth. Cut the wire into panels with a wire cutter and use J-clips and a J-clip tool to connect them—you can get both of these tools

at most feed stores. This type of cage allows droppings to fall through and therefore stays cleaner than a solid floor. You'll still need to hose down the bottom every other day or so. Provide a pan of sand in this cage to give the doves something to do.

This type of cage has the advantage of not being as high as the aviary, so the doves can't get any real momentum when they're scared and flying upward "through" the wire. The cage does, however, need to be protected on top, not only to keep the elements out, but also to prevent wild birds from perching on the top, potentially exposing your doves to disease.

You won't be able to get inside of this cage, so you'll have to buy a long-handled net in order to catch your doves for grooming, veterinary care, or in the case that you want to move them to another area. When you make your doors, hang a flap of wire on the inside of the door so that it's more difficult for your birds to escape should they come near the door when you're tending to them. Also, the lower the doors are, the less likely you'll have an escapee.

If you're not handy or don't have time to build this kind of cage, there are several companies that make very good cages just like this. These cages don't generally come with a shelter, so you'll have to put a slanted panel of wood or corrugated fiberglass on top and on the sides of part of the cage. They also don't come double-wired, so you'll have to do that when it arrives. Many dove keepers don't double-wire their cages, but I wouldn't risk the lives of my birds when it's so easy to just place another layer of wire on the cage, especially when there are known predators lurking about.

Nighttime predators, such as rats, snakes, raccoons, opossums, and weasels are particularly dangerous, though a tenacious cat can cause havoc as well. Mice won't really hurt the doves, though they can scare them at night, causing them to fly around in the darkness, which can lead to injury. Predators and mice can also bring disease into the aviary. It's better to keep the predators and pests out of the cage. Also, double wiring the cage or aviary will keep feral pigeons out of direct contact with your doves; feral pigeons are carriers of diseases that don't necessarily affect them, but are deadly to doves.

OUTDOOR AVIARY AND CAGE PLACEMENT

Place the aviary or cage as close to a sheltering side of the house or another structure as possible; avoid placing it next to the door, which may startle the doves every time it opens. Also avoid placing anything "scary" near the doves, such as a windsock, a loud wind chime, a garden whirligig, or other backyard decoration.

Avoid placing the aviary where it will receive many hours of afternoon sunlight. Doves can succumb to heat exposure, especially if the climate in your area tends to get very hot. Morning sunlight is good for doves, however, so wake up at sunrise one

A suspended cage should have a wire bottom so that the doves aren't exposed to their droppings. Make sure to clean the cage bottom every day. (Ringneck)

THE GUIDE TO OWNING A DOVE

morning during the aviary's planning stages and look for where the morning sun falls.

If your climate tends to be very cold—less than 32°F for long stretches—be sure to place the aviary in a place where drafts are uncommon, and make sure that the shelter is warm or at least very well protected from the elements.

Climate Control

In southern states or in particularly warm summers anywhere, you'll need a way to cool the aviary's shelter area if it's enclosed. Install a window with a wood or Plexiglas panel over a wire screen. This way you can open the window in the warm weather and close it in the cold weather. The Plexiglas also will let some light into the shelter where the birds might be nesting and tending to their young, and you'll be able to watch the birds inside the shelter without disturbing them. You can also install a small air-conditioning unit if you live in a very hot climate and have the proper, grounded electrical wiring leading to your aviary.

An aviary or large cage with an insulated shelter should be fine for keeping the doves warm all winter. You can also hang thick canvas cloth from the top of the aviary and tie it down each night like you would a tent, or you can cover the aviary with thick plastic at night and on very cold days to keep in some of the heat and keep out drafts. The plastic has the benefit of being

An insulated shelter in the cage or aviary should keep your doves warm during colder weather.

clear, though it tends to tear and will need to be replaced. If your area gets extremely cold, keep an eye on the water dishes to make sure that they don't freeze, or change them several times a day if they do.

If it's very cold where you live, keep only the hardier doves outdoors. Ringnecks, Bronzewings, Australian crested, Senegals, and Mournings should still thrive in colder temperatures, though many other doves will acclimate to colder weather as well. Avoid keeping tropical and subtropical doves in very cold weather. Young doves are particularly susceptible to the cold and can freeze to death. On particularly cold nights, you can collect the younger doves and bring them inside in a carrier or box, then return them to the aviary in the daylight. Be careful when handling the more timid species of doves, because they are known to die if overly frightened.

In the winter, you can use a plug-in portable radiator inside the aviary or bird room if you have grounded wiring and the unit has a safety shut-off feature, but never use a heater with exposed coils. Not only can it cause a fire, but many are also coated with a nonstick coating that creates a toxic fume that's deadly to birds. You can't use a heating source inside a cage, so you'll have to secure a double layer of plastic to the cage to keep cold drafts out and make sure that the water doesn't freeze.

INDOOR CAGES

If you're going to keep your smaller doves inside, choose the largest store-bought cage that you can afford and accommodate, at least 2x2x2 feet, though some people find that a cage of slightly smaller proportions works well for smaller doves if they are allowed time out of the cage. The length of the cage is most important—the doves will want to fly from side to side, so a rectangular cage is best. A round cage doesn't offer as much horizontal space and isn't as comfortable because there are no corners or walls that the dove can press up against when he feels threatened. Simple cages are best. Avoid antique cages with elaborate scrollwork, or tall cages shaped like pagodas or other similar structures.

A square cage, such as this one, provides more space and security than a round cage of the same size. (Tangerine Ringneck, female)

The tiny Diamond Dove does well in a smaller cage, though he will thrive in an aviary. (Diamond)

The best material for indoor caging is metal (preferably stainless steel or other nontoxic metal) and/or plastic. Both are easy to clean and disinfect and are long-lasting. Pet store cages are fine, as long as they are large enough. Do not put more than one pair of mature doves in a small indoor cage.

Some people dedicate a room to their doves or build or buy beautiful indoor aviaries. Some companies make cages that look like furniture enclosed in glass or Plexiglas rather than bars, making it easier to watch the doves. These cages often come with their own lighting and ventilation systems, but they are very expensive in proportion to the cost of the doves, and most people don't spend that much on indoor housing. Doves are relatively simple to keep, and you can either spend a fortune on them or go the inexpensive route—as long as they have enough space, food, water, grit, and sunlight (or artificial bird lighting), they won't care if they're in a $1,000 cage or a $10 cage.

Be sure that the doves can't stick their heads through the bars of the cage, and that the doors close securely. If you have other pets in the house, especially predators such as dogs, cats, rats, or snakes, make sure that the cage is in a place where it can't be tipped over and that the doors can't open if it does.

Perches and Ledges

The cage should have two different-sized perches and a roosting/nesting ledge. Don't place the perches or roosting ledge too high. If you're

All doves need either sunlight or special bird lighting to remain healthy. (Zebra)

breeding your doves in indoor cages (and most doves will breed, with or without your consent), you don't want to crowd the cage so that the male is unable to properly mount the female, a process that requires him to spread and flap his wings. Frustrated doves can become aggressive, resulting in bloodshed, so make the cage advantageous to breeding from the start.

Lighting

Indoor doves need lighting to remain healthy. Special bird bulbs providing full-spectrum light are an inexpensive substitute for sunlight, though these bulbs aren't as complete as sunlight. You can hang a tube-type bulb over the cage and place it on a timer to go on at dawn and off at dusk, or you can buy a lightbulb type and screw it into a spotlight trained on the cage.

If you use artificial lighting, make sure that you don't startle the doves by turning the lights on and off suddenly—going from pitch black to light and vice versa can cause undue stress. Instead, let the sunlight though a window wake the birds up before the light goes on and wait until it's naturally dark in the room before you turn off the lights. If the birds are in a basement, you can use dimmers to create the same effect. Even if you use these bulbs, setting your doves in the sun (supervised, of course!) on nice days for a few hours will do them a lot of good. Just make sure they don't overheat. Also, make sure they have enough water and that you place the cage in half sun/half shade so that they can move away from the light should they become too hot.

Air Purification

An air purifier, such as a HEPA filter, is the best investment you can make if you keep doves indoors. Doves are dusty and messy, and you'll thank me later for the recommendation. Misting the doves regularly or allowing them to take baths will cut down on the dust. You can also use an ionizer or humidifier, depending on your particular sensitivity issues.

Indoor Cage Placement

Where you place the cage depends a lot on the kind of interaction that you want to have with your doves. If you have a lone dove that you're taming into a hands-on pet, place the cage in a room that gets a lot of human traffic, such as the family room. If you have a pair that you tend to once a day, you can place them just about anywhere except the kitchen or bathroom, both rooms that tend to have fumes and temperature fluctuations.

Place the cage in an area that's easy to clean and where you're likely to be able to keep an eye on the doves in case there's ever a problem. The cage should be as high as possible because birds feel safer in a high spot where they can keep a lookout for danger. Never place the cage at ground level.

The cage can be close to a window, but should have some part of a wall or other solid area on at least one side of the cage. A predator outside or another disturbance can cause the doves to panic, so a safe spot where they can retreat is essential.

FOOD AND WATER IN THE AVIARY OR CAGE

If you're keeping multiple doves, you must place multiple feeding and watering stations in the cage with them. Some doves can become aggressive and not allow the less aggressive doves access to food and water. Also, place food and water at various levels of the cage, on the floor and at flight level.

In an aviary that's exposed to the elements (or even one that's not), you can use empty plastic milk containers as feeding stations. Simply cut an upward "D" shape into the jug on one side starting at about 3 inches from the bottom, fill it with seed, then hang it on the cage and/or place it on the floor. The doves will be able to stick their heads in to eat. Don't make the hole too large, or your doves will use the feeder as a nest. These feeders are great because they're cheap and disposable.

Commercial free-feeders and waterers are also great because you don't have to worry about the birds running out as often, and most keep the elements and defecation out of the inside of the container. A birdbath in the aviary is nice, but doves aren't the sharpest of

The "lone" dove kept as a companion should be housed in an area of the home where he will be sure to get enough attention. (Ringneck)

creatures and have been known to drown in even a shallow pool. If you choose to use a water bowl or bath, make sure to keep the water shallow and change it often. Water bottles are fine once the doves learn to use them, but I recommend against them as the sole source of water. Water bottles also tend to harbor bacteria in the spout if not cleaned well enough.

Whatever types of feeders and waterers you choose, make sure to clean them thoroughly at least three times a week with a 10-percent bleach solution and a scrub brush. Stainless steel and crockery are easiest to keep clean—plastic is easily scratched during cleaning and bacteria can grow in the crevasses and cause illness.

When you initially add doves to your large cage, find out where the feed and water containers were in the

Never put food and water containers below a perch, or else they will surely become soiled. (Tangerine Pearl Ringneck, female)

doves' last home. Place the feed and water in that area and then move them gradually toward the areas where you'd like to keep them. Make sure not to place food or water dishes beneath a perching area so that the contents don't become soiled.

You will also need a couple of small grit containers and larger bowls for veggies and other foods. Don't make your doves compete for these things, either. It shouldn't be "survival of the fittest" inside your aviary. Every bird should have a chance to live and be happy.

CLEANLINESS

Dirt doesn't cause disease, but pathogens can grow in dirty places, so keeping your doves' housing clean is extremely important. Moist spots can harbor bacteria or viruses that can make your doves ill or kill them. Some of the diseases that doves may contract are also contagious to humans, so keeping their housing clean is essential.

A 10- percent bleach solution is effective in killing most biological pathogens. Mix up the solution in a spray bottle, but be sure not to get the liquid near your doves, and rinse thoroughly after using it. An aviary or large outdoor cage should be hosed down daily in warmer weather and a couple of times a week in cold weather. (Scrape the droppings with a spackle knife in the meantime.) A stiff scrub brush is an essential cleaning item and should be used on all surfaces.

Perches should be kept very clean and should be disinfected at least twice a week. Rotating perches in and out of the cage, keeping one set out for cleaning while the other is in use, is a simple way to keep the perches very clean and allow them to dry out before placing them back inside the cage.

Clean the bottoms of indoor cages daily. Bird droppings dry and become airborne, which can cause illness in humans, especially if there are viruses and bacteria present. Always wash your hands well with antibacterial soap and hot water after handling your doves, or use an alcohol-based hand sanitizer.

ASSORTED ESSENTIAL ACCESSORIES

Scratching pan

If your outdoor doves have a concrete or wire floor as the bottom of their enclosure, they will like to have a pan of clean sand to scratch around in and even to rest in. A dove in a large enough indoor cage will enjoy a sand pan as well. Replace the sand every few days, or when it becomes soiled or moist.

Toys

Doves don't need toys the way other birds do. They're fine as long as they have a companion—either another dove or you—to keep them entertained.

Cage Cover

A dark, breathable fabric, such as a cotton sheet or black burlap, makes a good cage cover. Fitted custom cage

Perches are tough to keep clean, but scraping and washing them twice a week will help. (Tangerine Ringneck)

covers are nice because they block drafts well and keep out most of the light and potential disturbances.

THE CASE AGAINST FREE-FLYING DOVES

You can free fly pigeons, but you can't free fly doves. Pigeons have the instinct to return; most doves don't. If you've got pigeons, you can open your "coop" in the morning and then close it up in the early evening when the pigeons have returned. Don't try this with your "true" doves. Yes, there are services that let loose white "doves" at weddings and other events and those "doves" manage to find their way

Most doves should not be let outside of the cage for free flight unless provided with a safe, enclosed area. (Wild Pied Ringneck)

home. Those birds aren't really "doves" the way we're defining them here—they're pigeons. In other words, don't try this at home.

If you happen to have an escapee, buy a sparrow trap for smaller doves and a pigeon trap for larger doves or pigeons (available at most feed stores and online) and put the bird's mate (or a vocal friend of the opposite sex) safely inside the cage. The caged bird will call for its lost mate, which might be in hearing range and come down for a look and then make its way inside the trap. Make sure to put food and water inside the trap, too, and don't leave it unattended, or your lit-tle dove may just be a sitting duck for predators.

I recommend buying a kind of trap ahead of time so that you don't have to run around frantically looking for one when you need it. Also, you may want to trap a good-looking visitor to your yard that someone else lost. If you do manage to trap a bird of unknown origins, make sure to quarantine him and put up signs in your area for a lost bird. Let the local bird club know about the found bird as well, and record his leg band informa-tion, if he's wearing one—the owner can use this information to positively identify the bird, but realize that not every owner will have this information recorded.

Dove Nutrition and General Care

Doves aren't difficult to care for, but they do have specific requirements to keep them healthy. Most of the commonly kept doves are seed-eaters. The fruit doves are kept primarily by zoos and serious hobbyists interested in conservation. Their diet is difficult to replicate and most don't do very well in captivity unless their environment mimics their natural habitat. Therefore, we'll focus on feeding and caring for the seed-eaters in this chapter.

NUTRITION

Water

Clean, fresh water is the most important element of your dove's care. Doves are the only birds that can drink water without lifting the beak and thrusting the head back to swallow it. Therefore, your dove's water bowl should be at least 1.5 to 2 inches deep, but not much deeper. Change the water daily, and check it often to make sure it hasn't become fouled. Scrub the water container every day with a 10-percent bleach solution, making sure to rinse thoroughly, or have two sets of water containers that you rotate each day. The best water containers for doves have a hood or cover so that the doves can't easily soil the water. Some dove keepers add a few drops of apple cider vinegar to the water. This retards the growth of bacteria and is healthful in general.

Seed

The staple diet for most doves is seed. Unlike other birds, doves swallow seeds whole, so you'll always know when your birds have run out. Most feed stores or pet stores have dove seed mixes that are fine and easy to use. Diamond Doves use a finch seed and will reject the larger seeds in a dove mix.

Recycled gallon jugs make great feed containers, as seen here with these Ringneck Doves. (Fawn Ringneck, male)

For outdoor doves, you should start adding oily seeds and legumes to their diet, such as sunflower and shelled peanut in the fall to beef up the birds before winter. Discontinue these seeds in the spring to make sure that the birds don't become overweight.

If you can't find a specific dove mix, you can make your own mix from separate seeds or ready-made hookbill and canary mixes from the pet store. Try your doves on a variety of seeds to see which ones they prefer. This way you won't waste your money on seeds that your birds won't eat. Most doves, however, love millet spray, which you can offer a couple of times a week.

Most doves can be allowed to feed at will, so you don't have to ration out seed—simply fill up the food contain-

ers and you'll eventually be able to gauge how much your doves eat a day and feed just slightly over that amount. Doves with nestlings may eat more, so take that into consideration when doling out food.

Vitamins and Minerals

As I mentioned earlier, vitamins in the water will only serve to foul it unless you change it several times daily. Instead, you should add oil-based and/or powdered vitamins to the birdseed. Seed does not contain the appropriate vitamins and minerals that your dove needs, so you must supplement it.

Mixing in a calcium powder, such as one made for horses (available at your local feed store or online) is great for laying hens or hens getting ready for breeding season. You can also scrape a cuttlebone or mineral block over the seed for added calcium, but don't hang these items in the cage because your doves won't be able to use them in their solid forms. Livestock salt with trace elements is also good for breeding birds and can be sprinkled on the feed twice a week.

Human-grade high-end supplements, such as powdered spirulina, barley grass, bee pollen, and acidophilus, are also great for doves and will keep them in prime condition. You can offer these mixed in with egg food or other soft foods.

Manufactured Diet

Pellets are a wholly manufactured diet based on a diet used for poultry. I recommend pellets and commercial crumbles as an addition to the diet but not as the staple of the diet. Most of these pellets are made for "game birds," that is, birds that are meant for sport, not to live as a long-time companion in a home. I recommend mixing the pellets or crumbles with the seed or offering them in a separate dish, but pellets should not be the sole diet for doves.

Grit

Most dove keepers agree that grit is important for digestion and is a good calcium source. There are two kinds of grit: indigestible and digestible. Indigestible grit is primarily sand and ground-up stone. Digestible grit is calcium-based and is usually made from ground-up oyster shells, eggshells, and/or cuttlebone. Doves have a digestive organ called the gizzard (ventriculus), which grinds up the hard food that they eat, and the grit helps with this grinding process. Indigestible grit should be offered in very small amounts, but a cup of digestible grit can be offered freely. Most types of grit can be found at your local pet shop. Offer grit in a separate dish and change it if it becomes moist or soiled.

Fresh Foods

Doves should have shredded, dark, leafy greens three times a week, but cut back if you notice severely runny droppings. A variety of thoroughly washed and dried greens, such as dandelions, spinach, kale, and carrot or beet tops are healthy for your doves.

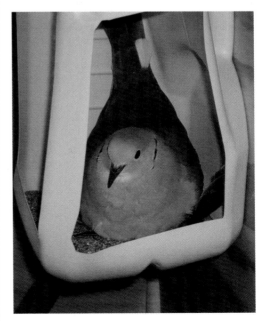

If you use large containers as feeders, be aware that your doves may try to use them as nests. (Wild Type Ringneck, male)

Grated carrots, apple, and pear are often relished too. Frozen (defrosted) or fresh peas are a favorite of the larger doves and pigeons, as are berries and corn cut off the cob.

Other Foods

Hardboiled egg makes a great treat and rearing food for nesting parents with hatchlings. Boil the eggs for over half an hour to kill any potential bacteria that can transmit disease to your birds, then crush the egg, shell and all, and offer it in a separate dish. Commercial egg food is also a good supplement for breeding doves and can be mixed with the hardboiled egg.

Cooked cereals, such as oatmeal and small-sized pastas, are good treats for your doves, especially if you fortify them with vitamins and minerals— serve warm but not hot. You can bake corn muffins for your doves too, adding greens, shredded carrots, seeds, vitamins, minerals, and anything else your doves enjoy. Freeze and defrost as needed.

Whole-wheat breads are good treats, as are bran muffins (without sugar), whole-wheat crackers, and other healthy grain items.

Make sure to remove all cooked and fresh foods a couple of hours after offering them in warm weather, and no more than eight hours later in cold weather. Spoiled foods can cause your doves to become very ill.

Live Food

Many doves really enjoy mealworms, which are a great source of protein, especially during the winter and when nesting and rearing young. Some pet shops sell mealworms, or you can order them online. Offer each dove no more than five worms three times a week. Some softbill foods contain insects, or you can buy flies and other dried insects (sold in the turtle or reptile section) as a treat for your doves.

GENERAL CARE

Bathing

Most outdoor doves bathe without encouragement in a shallow bath or in a mist of water from a sprinkler. In warm weather, offer your doves a bath every day. Some indoor doves will bathe themselves readily, but some won't. Because doves are dusty and bathing is healthy, mist your indoor doves a couple of times a week in warm weather and allow the bird to dry on its own. In colder weather, you can blow-dry the bird using a semi-warm setting and holding the dryer a couple of feet away from the bird, waving the air back and forth over the bird's body. Do not overheat the bird!

Unless your dove is extremely dirty for some extraordinary reason, you don't need to do more than mist him. Misting will cause the bird to preen, an action which cleans the feathers naturally. If, for some reason, the bird is filthy because he got into something or was ill and has feces stuck to his feathers, you can bathe the bird gently and quickly in the sink using a mild baby shampoo, making sure to wash with the grain of the feathers, not against them. Do not wash the bird's face or head, and make sure that the water is lukewarm. Dry the bird thoroughly with a towel and/or blow dryer and keep him out of drafts. Never leave him alone in the sink with the water, and never overheat him—I can't stress that enough.

A lot of doves like to bathe in wet grass or greens, so you can also offer a patch of wet sod or a platter of really wet greens for the doves to bathe in, especially if there's a mister or sprinkler over the grass and the sun is out. The water can be directed into the part of the aviary where the sod or greens are placed.

Exercise

The best exercise for doves, or any bird, is flying. It's what they do naturally, and it keeps them fit. Doves kept in aviaries or large cages have no problem staying in shape. However, doves in smaller cages tend to become obese if they aren't let out for some exercise or if they're fed a diet too high in fat. Seeds are very fatty, so feed more fresh foods to sedentary doves and restrict seed to the amount that your dove can consume in ten minutes, three times a day. Put the seed bowl inside the cage and then remove it after the specified time. Doves should never be without food,

however, so leave the less-caloric foods inside the cage. Never restrict breeding doves or those caring for babies.

Sleep

Doves begin to roost around dusk and then don't move during the night. They wake early in the morning and begin cooing and calling. If you don't want to wake up that early, covering the cage with a dark cloth should help.

If your doves are interrupted in their sleep by sudden light or noise, they can erupt in fright, flying recklessly around the cage or aviary, and can hurt themselves. Avoid disturbing them whenever possible. Having a nightlight on in the doves' area may help to avoid the "night frights."

Wing Clipping

Clipping a bird's wings allows him to fly gently to the floor instead of taking off into the wild blue yonder. While wing clipping is a common and accept-

Fully-flighted doves are strong, competent flyers, so make sure your dove is protected from open windows or doors. (Pink Ringneck, female)

ed practice, there is some evidence that clipping a bird's wings does frustrate the bird and can create some health problems, including obesity, if the bird is not active enough.

If you feel guilty about having your bird's wings clipped, you're not alone. Many people feel that wing clipping is cruel or that it hurts the bird. In truth, when done properly, clipping wings hurts as little as a haircut; the feathers, like hair, grow back in about five months if the bird is healthy, perhaps even sooner.

If you've chosen to clip your dove's wing feathers to prevent him from flying away, you should find a professional in your area who will clip them at first and show you how to do it your-

self. Many owners are squeamish about clipping their own bird's wings and choose to have someone else do it for them. If you have an avian veterinarian, he or she is the best person to clip wings until you learn to do it safely yourself.

To clip safely, grasp the bird around the neck and the back, leaving the chest free. Your thumb is on one side of the bird's neck, bracing the bottom of his jaw, and your index finger is on the other side, doing the same. The bird should look like he's resting with his back in your palm. Be gentle!

Once you feel that you're holding your dove properly, have someone else gently extend his wing and clip the first seven feathers (the long ones

Here you can see the flight feathers beneath the primary coverts—the flight feathers are the first seven long feathers starting at the outside of the wing.

After a bird molts, his feathers grow back, and you have to re-clip the wings. (Rosy Ringneck)

at the end of the wing), beginning at the point where the primary feather coverts end—those are the feathers on the upper side of the wing that end at the midpoint of the primary flight feathers. With a sharp scissor, clip each feather, one by one, making a clean snip. Clip both wings.

Molting

When birds molt, they shed their feathers and make way for new ones to grow. The old feathers may have become ragged and not useful for insulation or flying anymore. A molt can happen once or twice a year, depending on the amount of light and warmth your dove is exposed to, and

it is a very stressful time for a bird. The newly growing feathers can be uncomfortable or tender.

You will notice little "pins" beginning to poke out from between your dove's other feathers. These are called pinfeathers. The "pin" is a sheath of material (keratin) that protects the new feather until it is ready to emerge. Molting birds do not lose all of their feathers at once. Most molts range from a few weeks to several months long, and feathers are replaced gradually. If you notice bald patches on your dove's body or if his feathers become so thin you can see the skin beneath them, take your bird to your avian vet-

Even if your dove's feathers are healthy, broken blood feathers can still emerge and should be pulled out with a pair of needle-nosed pliers. (Tangerine Ringneck)

erinarian right away—there may be a serious problem.

Pinfeathers and new feathers that have just emerged from the sheath have a blood supply and will bleed if injured or broken. This often happens with a wing feather, especially in a clipped bird that does not have fully grown wing feathers that would protect a new feather from breaking. If you notice a bleeding feather, perhaps one that was clipped during wing trimming, don't panic. Pull the feather straight out from the root with one quick motion and the bleeding will stop immediately. A pair of needle-nosed pliers is good for this purpose, and should be kept in your bird first-aid kit. If you're squeamish about this, apply styptic powder to the bleeding area and take your bird to your avian veterinarian as soon as possible.

THE GUIDE TO OWNING A DOVE

Dove Behavior and Handling

Most of the commonly kept doves will exhibit the same types of behaviors, more or less. The following section describes some of the behaviors you might see and what they mean.

COMMON DOVE BEHAVIORS

Vocalization

Doves aren't loud, but they are persistent in their cooing, especially when they're in breeding mode. Not all doves sound the same, and if you choose to house several different types of doves, you will come to recognize their distinct voices.

The more doves you have, the louder and more persistent they are—multiple doves vocalize over each other and will be louder when they are all together. Generally, the noise is only bothersome to people who are very sensitive to sound, but neighbors usually won't complain about it.

Preening

A bird preens by running his beak through his feathers, making sure they're all clean and in place. Each feather is made up of little strands that zip together like Velcro—your

Doves aren't loud birds, but they are persistent enough in their vocalizations to irritate those with sensitive hearing. (Rosy Silky Ringneck, male)

A frightened dove will sometimes freeze in place, but more often he will fly upward—fast! (Cape)

dove will spend a lot of time making sure that each feather is zipped properly. Healthy doves preen frequently every day—ill doves may stop preening and look a little disheveled. Doves also preen each other (allopreening), which can indicate mate bonding or contact between parent and squab (baby dove).

Ruffle Fluffle

After preening, usually before and after a nap, and before and after embarking on a new task (flying to a perch, eating, etc.) a dove may give his feathers a quick little "ruffle fluffle"—fluffing the feathers quickly, then smoothing them down again. After preening, he does this to remove all the debris he has just dislodged from his feathers; other times, the dove ruffles to release tension.

Bowing and Cooing

This is typical behavior for a male dove with his eye on a mate. He will puff up his chest and walk around the hen, bowing and cooing to get her attention. Females will occasionally exhibit this behavior, but not often.

Challenge posture

The challenge posture is usually seen in doves defending their mate, nest, or squabs. The head is held low into the body and the rump feathers are raised, kind of like hackles on a dog.

Fear posture

A fearful dove will sometimes "freeze"—stand tall and still, his neck craned and feathers close to his body, so as to prevent a "predator" from seeing him.

Fear Flight

A dove that is frightened suddenly

will usually fly straight up, blindly. This can be dangerous to doves in an aviary, because they may get some momentum going and crash into the aviary's ceiling. Hang some mesh or place soft, easily cleaned padding on the top of the aviary to avoid injury.

Dove Intelligence

Doves aren't known as the brains of the bird world. They won't learn elaborate tricks (or any tricks, for that matter), and most people are happy just to sit and watch them interact or to have their pet dove perched on their hand or shoulder. The dove is no dummy, however. Individual doves do come to know their human family and will accept them as part of their flock. A male that's very bonded to his human "flock" may even do a mating dance to a human family member. This doesn't mean that he's dumb—he's just programmed to behave this way.

Even a tame dove will become frightened of certain things, such as their human wearing a new hat, loud noises, and severe changes in wardrobe. Move slowly and deliberately around your doves and offer them treats from your hand. They'll soon tame down if they come to realize that your presence and tasty treats go together.

HANDLING

Most doves take well to hand taming, especially if they've had contact with humans from the time they hatched. Many people don't clip their doves' wings, but it may be necessary during the hand-taming process—the wing feathers will grow out after the bird molts (the natural process of losing feathers to grow new ones). This happens once or twice a year, depending on the weather. When you clip your dove, clip only the last seven feathers (the flight feathers) halfway up the wing. Clipping is also used on aggressive birds in an aviary setting, but the clip is less severe and slows the bird down instead of grounding him. It's best to have someone who knows how to clip show you before you do it on your own.

Begin earning your dove's trust by offering him tasty treats like mealworms for a few days. Once he seems at home, gently take him out of the cage, bring him to a small

This 16-day-old fledgling is already comfortable being hand-tamed and will remain so if handled regularly. (White Ringneck)

Gentle handling and treats soon earn a dove's trust. This juvenile female is obviously fond of her human friend. (White Ringneck, female)

room, and sit down on the floor. Then, gently place him on your finger while offering a treat. If the dove flies off your hand, retrieve him and place him on your finger again. Move slowly and deliberately. If he won't stay on your hand, sit with your knees bent and put him on one of your knees, offering him treats. Do this for a few minutes a day, every day, and make the session enjoyable.

Eye contact can be threatening for a dove. A prey animal that assumes any animal with eyes on the front of its head is going to eat him, don't stare directly at a skittish dove when you're trying to tame him. Don't "shush" a dove to calm him as you would a child, because you may sound like a snake, one of the dove's natural predators.

Imagine life though your dove's eyes when you're taming him. Even doves living in pairs or in an aviary with multiple birds can become quite tame if your taming methods are gentle and account for the dove's sometimes wary character.

Your Healthy Dove

Doves are hardy birds, thriving in just about every climate on earth. They aren't as fragile as they look, but doves in captivity are prone to certain illnesses and accidents that they wouldn't necessarily meet in their natural habitat. This chapter covers common ailments and accidents, as well as how to help a dove should these occur. If you suspect your dove is suf-

Keeping doves healthy is easy if you understand their proper care and learn to recognize signs of illness. (Cream Pied Ringneck)

fering from any of these ailments, take him to his veterinarian immediately.

VETERINARY CARE

Your bird should have access to a knowledgeable veterinarian when he needs it, and finding an avian veterinarian is probably the best option for your dove. An avian veterinarian specializes in the care and treatment of birds, has trained on birds, and treats birds on a regular basis. A regular veterinarian can treat some bird ailments, but an avian veterinarian sees all kinds of avian illnesses and injuries and is better able to diagnose and treat these problems. The office of an avian veterinarian will be equipped with the latest technology for diagnosing and treating birds of all kinds.

If you live in or near a large city, you should have no problem finding a doctor specializing in birds. You may have to travel a bit farther if you live in a rural area. You can find an avian veterinarian near you by checking out the Association of Avian Veterinarians at www.aav.org. You may also contact the American Federation of Aviculture at www.afa.birds.org. See the Resources section on the end of this book for more information.

SIGNS AND SYMPTOMS OF A SICK DOVE

A major part of making sure your dove remains healthy is by being an observant owner. Make an effort to get to know your bird's everyday, healthy behavior—this way you'll be better able to tell when something's wrong. It's often difficult to tell if a bird is sick until he is very sick, but an observant owner will be able to see the signs early. The following are some signs of illness in doves.

Excessive sleeping

An ill dove may sleep too much, especially during the day. Sleeping on the bottom of the cage is a particularly significant symptom unless it's the dove's habit to do so.

Fluffed-up Appearance

Birds keep their feathers fluffed to retain heat close to the skin when they're cold and when they're ill. A fluffed-up and ill bird will be inactive and look a little hunkered down as well. He will not look sleek the way doves do when they're well.

Loss of Appetite

You should know how much food and what types of food your dove consumes each day. Loss of appetite or diminished appetite could indicate illness.

Change in attitude

If your dove seems listless and is not behaving in his usual manner, call your veterinarian.

Lameness

If your dove can't use his feet, there's something very wrong—illness, poisoning, or an injury might be responsible.

Panting or labored breathing

Doves have a very sensitive respira-

Paying attention to your dove's normal, everyday behavior will alert you to signs of illness. (Ivory White Silky Ringneck, male)

tory system and are susceptible to airborne irritants, such as aerosol sprays, fumes from heated nonstick cookware, and tobacco smoke. Always keep your dove away from fumes and airborne toxins. If you notice your dove panting or having respiratory distress, call your avian veterinarian right away. Changes in breathing, bubbling from the mouth or nostrils, and tail-bobbing may signify a respiratory illness or overheating.

Discharge

Discharge from the eyes, nares (nostrils), or vent may indicate illness.

Bubbling from the nares may also indicate a problem, so if you see any of these symptoms, contact your vet immediately.

Debris around the face or on feathers

Debris in these places indicates poor grooming or regurgitation—potential signs of illness.

Swollen eyelids and cloudy eyes

Doves have a third eyelid that helps keep the eye healthy by brushing away debris. A dove with an eye problem may squint or scratch the eye. Any eye condition must be treated immediately.

Overgrown beak

An overgrown beak may indicate a

nutritional disorder or other illness or injury. Take your pet to an avian veterinarian for treatment.

Change in droppings

Your dove's droppings should consist of a solid green portion, white urates (over the green part), and a clear liquid. If the droppings are discolored (very dark green, black, yellow, or red) and there has been no change in diet, there might be a problem. Also, if there's a pungent odor or if the droppings seem far more liquid than usual, call your veterinarian immediately. Doves that are about a day or so away from laying an egg will have large, patty-like droppings—this is normal, and it goes away after the egg has been laid.

TYPICAL ILLNESSES

The following is a short list of illnesses typical to doves (and pigeons). This is not a complete list, nor does it take the place of consulting with your avian veterinarian. Many illnesses that affect doves have similar symptoms but are treated much differently. It's important to know what disease you're dealing with before you treat the problems, and this is where a good avian veterinarian becomes necessary. Remember that keeping your doves' housing very clean and always quarantining new birds goes a long way toward keeping your birds healthy. All of the following illnesses require immediate veterinary care.

Salmonella

Symptoms of salmonella include green, loose droppings, compromised balance, paralysis, and even death of the babies in the nest. Symptoms vary—this destructive illness needs immediate veterinary care for all birds exposed to it.

Psittacosis

The symptoms for psittacosis, also called "Parrot Fever," include general poor condition, lameness, difficulty breathing, smelly droppings, and distended abdomen. This disease is highly contagious among birds and is also contagious to humans, where it causes pneumonia-like symptoms.

Streptococcus

Symptoms of streptococcus include labored breathing, fluffiness, inactivity, weight loss, and green droppings. Requires treatment with antibiotics.

Newcastle Disease

Newcastle disease is a type of paramyxovirus. Symptoms include turned neck, thirst, watery droppings, and compromised balance. The disease is very contagious and fatal, but some birds recover. Pigeons and doves can be vaccinated against this disease every year from one month of age.

Coccidiosis

Symptoms of this disease range from general listlessness to extreme thirst and mucous-filled diarrhea.

Pox

This is a virus caused by mosquitoes biting doves that are kept outside. In the dry form of the disease, small bumps grow on the fleshy parts of the body; in the wet form, there can be cankers inside the mouth. Unfortunately, this disease is usually fatal, especially in the wet form.

Aspergillosis

Caused by fungi, panting, coughing, sneezing, nasal discharge, and swollen joints could indicate that your bird has aspergillosis, a condition caused by a mold growing in the aviary or cage, either in the feed or in damp spots.

Fungi grow in damp, unclean places in the aviary or cage, even in food dishes, and can cause respiratory and digestive illness. Cleanliness should keep most fungi at bay.

Candida

This yeast-like infection, which can be fatal but easily cured if caught early, is caused by dampness in the aviary, damp feed, and mold. Symptoms include a slick, mucus coating in the throat and digestive difficulties.

Parasites

Parasites—which include lice and fleas—are easily treated once diagnosed. In many cases, they are due to unclean conditions and overcrowding.

Roundworms

Roundworms are parasites that live freely in the intestines and rob the dove of nutrients. Symptoms include gradual weight loss, anemia, diarrhea, listlessness, and dull feathers. The condition is very contagious. Many people who keep large numbers of doves or pigeons regularly treat them for roundworm.

Threadworms

These worms bury into the intestine wall and can lead to blood loss and weight loss. Symptoms include gradual weight loss, anemia, diarrhea, listlessness, and dull feathers.

Bloodmites (redmites)

These little mites live in the crevices of the aviary during the day and come out at night to feed on the doves, particularly on youngsters. They can cause anemia, and in the case of a rampant infestation, even death. The aviary should be cleaned with a bleach solution and Sevin Dust (which you can buy at any nursery or hardware store) sprinkled liberally around nesting areas. Sevin Dust is harmless to the birds and will keep away many insects and parasites.

Going Light

The term "going light" simply means that the dove is becoming very thin for an unknown reason. The bird may be ill with one of the above ailments and will regain some weight with treatment. Sometimes, "going light" is a result of general digestive problems stemming from not enough good bacteria in the gut. Offering regular doses of acidophilus, which you can find in a powdered form in health food stores, should help. Consult your veterinarian for treatment of this condition.

Frostbite

Frostbite may cause the loss of toes

and feet and can even cause death. If you keep your doves outdoors during the cold time of year, consider bringing them inside on the coldest nights. The frostbitten area will eventually die and the flesh will change to a dark color. If you discover the condition early enough, you can place your bird in a warm hospital cage and call the veterinarian immediately. If you catch the condition at the point where the flesh has turned dark, take your bird to the avian veterinarian as soon as possible—this bird is in grave danger.

Overheating

If you notice your dove panting, standing with his wings open, or lying on the floor of the cage or aviary, he may be overcome by the heat. Keep a spray bottle handy and lightly mist the bird with cool water, repeating the misting until he's soaked to the skin. Watch him closely until his attitude seems normal. If your dove does not respond to the cool misting, remove him from the warm spot immediately and place him in a cooler location. If you have a fan, place the flow of air on the cage and mist him again—as he recovers, move the flow of air from directly hitting the cage. Dip the bird's beak into a shallow dish of water to see if he will drink. Don't force him. Call your avian veterinarian right away.

In warm weather, make sure that your birds always have cool water to drink. Doves absolutely should not be kept in full sunlight unless they have a shaded spot where they can get out of the sun.

Loss of Consciousness

An unconscious bird may be suffering from a toxin in the air—ventilate the room well and try to revive your bird by taking him to a different area of the home. If he doesn't revive quickly, contact your avian veterinarian right away.

Broken bones

While a dove's bones are strong enough to allow the movement of wings during flight, the bones are easily broken. Some of the bones contain air sacs that aid in breathing, and can cause a severe respiratory problem when broken. See your veterinarian immediately if you suspect that your dove has a broken bone.

Egg-Bound Hen

An egg-bound hen has trouble passing an egg, a condition that can be deadly. You will notice a swelling in her abdomen and may notice other symptoms of distress, such as leg paralysis. Place her in the hospital cage with a good deal of humidity (a warm water humidifier or professional brooder is great for this) and warmth up to 90°F for a few hours. If your dove does not pass the egg within a few hours and you can't get to your avian veterinarian right away, place a few drops of mineral oil (or olive oil) in her vent and a few drops in her mouth with an eye dropper—this may help her to pass the egg. Either way, take her to the veterinarian as soon as possible for an examination.

A dove's clean, tight feathers provide warmth and protection from the elements. If you notice a drastic change in feather quality, there could be a health problem. (Ash Pearled Ringneck)

Broken Blood Feathers and Bleeding Nails

A broken feather that has a blood supply (blood feather) or a bleeding nail is a small wound and can often be treated successfully at home. Keep some styptic power or a styptic pen on hand and apply a small pinch of the styptic powder directly to the wound—this should stop the bleeding immediately. Regular baking flour works well in a pinch. Note: Not all feathers have a blood supply, just the feathers that haven't grown all the way in yet.

Oil on the Feathers

Oil on the feathers makes it impos-sible for a bird to regulate his body temperature and is a serious condi-tion. Feathers keep heat near the skin when the bird is cold—if they are cov-ered in oil, they become ineffective at this. If your bird gets soaked in oil, you can dust him with flour or corn-starch, blot him with paper towels, then give him a warm bath in a tub filled with warm water and some very mild, grease-fighting dish soap. Do not scrub the bird—simply allow him to soak and repeat the bath several times. Place him in a warm hospital cage and take him to the avian veteri-narian as soon as possible.

Contact with Poison

Bird proofing your home should help to eliminate the danger of poisoning; however, accidents can occur even in the best of circumstances. If you believe that your dove has come into contact with poison, call your veterinarian immediately and then call the National Animal Poison Control Center 24-hour Poison Hotline at (800) 548-2423, (888) 4-ANIHELP or (900) 680-0000. You can also call the ASPCA's Animal Poison Control Center at 888-426-4435. Both charge a small fee.

Fractures, Beak, Eye, and Foot Injuries, and Seizures

Fractures, beak, eye, and foot injuries, and seizures are all cause for calling your avian veterinarian right away and rushing to the office for treatment. In the meantime, place your dove in a warm hospital cage and make him comfortable. Transport him in a hospital cage if you can.

FIRST-AID KIT FOR BIRDS

You should always have a dove first-aid kit on hand for any emergency. It's not a great idea to treat a serious emergency yourself, but in some cases the veterinarian (or experienced dove hobbyist) might "talk you through" a procedure on the phone. The following is a list of contents that every dove first-aid kit should contain:

- Antibiotic ointment (for small wounds, non-greasy—oil prevents a bird from keeping in his body heat)
- Eyewash
- Bandages and gauze
- Bottled water (you may need clean, fresh water to flush out a wound or clean your bird)
- Baby bird formula (can be used for adults that are having a difficult time eating)
- Cotton balls
- Cotton swabs
- Non-greasy first-aid lotion
- Dishwashing detergent (mild)
- Heating pad (always allow a bird the option of moving off of a heating pad)
- Hydrogen peroxide (always use in a weak solution with water)
- Nail clippers
- Nail file
- Needle-nosed pliers (for broken blood feathers)
- Penlight
- Pedialyte, or similar (great for reviving a weak bird)
- Saline solution
- Sanitary wipes
- Sharp scissors
- Syringe (without needle)
- Styptic powder (to stop bleeding)
- Small, clean towels (for holding or swabbing)
- Spray bottle (for misting)
- Alcohol (for tools)
- Tweezers
- Transport cage
- Veterinarian's telephone number

It's also a good idea to include a sealed bag or can of your bird's base diet in the kit in case an emergency forces you and your bird out of your home.

MAKING A HOSPITAL CAGE

A hospital cage is essential for comforting an ill or injured bird. Your dove's regular cage may contain other birds and might not be warm enough. A 10-gallon fish tank or medium-sized, plastic critter-keeper or carrier lined with paper towels makes a great hospital cage. Place a screen on top and a dark towel covering one-half to three-fourths of the cage's top and sides—do not cover the entire cage with the towel. Place a heating pad on medium heat under half of the cage—your dove should have the option of moving away from the heat. Place seeds and millet spray in the cage, as well as a very shallow dish of water—a weak bird can drown in even a half an inch of water.

Do not place perches in the cage. Place a rolled-up hand towel in one corner so that your bird can perch or snuggle up to it if he wants to. Place the hospital cage in a quiet, safe place where your bird can recuperate undisturbed.

THE DANGER OF HUMAN MEDICINES

Never give your dove human medicine unless directed to do so by a veterinarian. Many human medicines are toxic and deadly to birds. Some experienced bird keepers do use human medicine to treat simple ailments in their doves, but I'm reluctant to advise it because of dosing and weight issues, and also because the average person may not be able to correctly diagnose what ailment the dove may have.

Breeding
Your Dove

Most doves are easy to breed and, in fact, won't wait for you to set them up for breeding. This chapter gives the basics on breeding doves, though each species has its own quirks and needs. You should research your par-

With most of the common dove species, it is nearly impossible to distinguish between the sexes until the birds have paired up. (White Ringnecks)

ticular species before embarking on a breeding program.

DISTINGUISHING THE SEX OF YOUR DOVES

Most of the commonly kept doves are difficult to sex until they reach maturity and begin behaving like adults. Before then, it's anybody's guess. However, there are some decent ways to distinguish sex. First of all, only females lay eggs. If you've got a bird laying eggs, it's definitely a hen.

Females will have wider and blunter hipbones surrounding the vent. Hold the bird upside-down, and feel gently around the vent. If the hipbones are close together and pointy, you may have a male. (This method works some of the time, but not always.)

Compared to a female, a male may have a flatter, squarer head and a wider beak. Males are almost always larger than females.

Some mutations are "sex linked," meaning that a certain color or trait is determined by the sex of the bird and can only occur in that sex under a specific pairing of a male and a female. If your dove's breeder is good at genetics, you'll often know from the start what sex your birds are.

With Diamond Doves, the mature male's eyering is generally thicker than the female's.

Mature males do a little dance called the "bow coo." He bows his head repeatedly and coos to his beloved. Females will do this as well, but not often.

Females crouch down and spread their wings about one-third of the way to the side, inviting the male to copulate with her. Then, a male will often feed a female by taking her beak inside his. A male will "drive" a female about to lay eggs to the nest, where she can't flirt with other males.

THE BREEDING PROCESS

Start with an unrelated pair of at least six months of age, though I recommend you wait a year before breeding your hens. Some breeders mate related birds, but it's risky. For best results, especially for your first pair, start with the healthiest, unrelated birds you can find.

Doves will try to build a nest, but they're not very good at it. Therefore,

Determining the sexes of these young doves will be difficult until they become older.

you must provide a nest. It can be as simple as a breeding box that you buy from a feed store, a flowerpot, a sturdy bowl, wire baskets, or any other open container that you feel would be appropriate. Just place at least 2 inches of pine shavings and straw at the bottom of the item you select as the nest and place the item high in an aviary or at the bottom of a smaller cage if there's not a lot of headroom.

The male will do a mating dance for the female, full of bowing, cooing, wing flapping, and stalking. He will strut around, trying to get her attention, tail spread. Eventually, if the male and female are a true pair (opposite sex doves that like each other and are willing to breed), she will return his affections and they will mate, him mounting her and pressing his vent against hers.

The hen will lay one egg about ten days after copulation and the next egg about two days later. Once the second egg is laid, the parents will begin sharing incubation duty, the male during the day and the female at night, more or less. About 18 days later, the first egg will hatch, followed by the second a few hours to two days later. If there are two babies, chances are that one is male and the other female.

Feeding the Parents

All along, you should have been providing the parents with nutritious food, including lots of protein foods like eggs and mealworms. Once the eggs hatch, continue providing these foods along with soft, nutritious foods like bread soaked in soymilk and egg food. The parents create a protein-rich "pigeon milk" in their crops (the crop is the organ that holds the food before it goes to the gizzard – kind of akin to the stomach) and feed this to the babies for the first ten days or so, when they begin feeding regurgitated food.

Note the pin feathers on these chicks—the new feathers are still in their sheathes. This is particularly noticeable in the feathers of the light-colored chick on the left.

Babies are called "squabs" when they're hairless and "squeakers" when they begin to feather out. They generally fledge (leave the nest) at about 35 days. The parents will have, in the meantime, bred again, and will have babies ready to hatch. They will not want the big, feathered babies around and may become aggressive toward them. Remove the babies as soon as they're eating well on their own.

Banding the Babies

Bands around the dove's leg offer identification for you, and some states even require them. Babies can be banded when they are about seven days old, when the foot is small enough to go through the band, but not too small that it will slip off. The band is often inscribed with the year of hatching, your state, a number unique to the baby, club identification, and your initials should you choose to have them on it.

Be very gentle with the babies when you band them—handle them on a counter over a towel and return them to the nest as quickly as possible. Use petroleum jelly to grease the foot and the band, and use a toothpick to help slide the first three toes through the band, followed by the last toe, which you will have to gently pry out of the band. The band should be on the bird's ankle—not on the elbow. Do not push the band further to get the last toe out of it—simply work it gently with the toothpick.

This parent dove is taking care of her squab and another egg waiting to hatch. (Tangerine Ringneck)

Always band the babies at dusk, so that the parent birds don't have all day to try to pick the band off. When you buy your bands (there are suppliers on the Internet or you can get them at some feed stores or your local dove club), make absolutely sure to get the right size.

HAND-FEEDING

Occasionally, you will have to hand-feed a baby dove if his parents are neglectful or die, or if you find one in the wild. Unlike other birds that open their mouths for feeding and wait for the parent to put something in it, the baby dove puts its beak inside the parent's beak. For this reason, you can't hand-feed baby doves the way you might hand-feed a parrot. They don't like having food put into their mouths. There's an easy solution. Fill a rubber glove with baby formula, which you can buy at any pet shop and make according to the directions, snip a tiny hole in one of the fingers, and stick the baby's beak through the hole. He will soon get the idea.

If you don't have hand-feeding formula on hand and you're in a pinch, you can soak whole-wheat bread, cereal, baby cereal, and other similar items in soymilk (or even water), and follow the above directions.

Never feed a cold baby—this can cause crop stasis, which can lead to

These cute, little squabs are just the right age for banding.

death. Babies should be warmed in a brooder or hospital cage before you feed them. Also, make absolutely sure that the hand-feeding formula isn't too hot. Feed very slowly and in small amounts so that you don't choke the baby. Fill the baby's crop—you'll see the sac at the base of its neck fill up—but don't stuff it. The food can back up and the baby can die.

IN A PERFECT WORLD

In a perfect world, breeding doves would be uncomplicated. However, things don't go according to plan sometimes—mates are aggressive to each other, other birds in the aviary will bother the pair, the parents will scramble the eggs or squash the babies, and any number of other failure scenarios might occur. If you don't want your pair to breed, you can put dummy eggs in their nest or you can separate the sexes, though doves are happiest in mixed pairs.

I hope that this book has given you a little taste of what it's like to own doves and has shown you how to take care of them well. If you would like to learn more about them as you care for them, I strongly recommend that you join a dove society or a bird club. Good luck with your birds of peace.

Resources

MAGAZINES

Bird Talk
Fancy Publications, Inc.
3 Burroughs
Irvine, CA 92618
Phone: (949) 855-8822
Fax: (949) 855-3045
Website: www.birdtalk.com

Bird Times
Pet Publishing, Inc.
7-L Dundas Circle
Greensboro, NC 27407
Phone: (336) 292-4047
Fax: (336) 292-4272
E-mail: btsubscription@petpublishing.com
Website: www.birdtimes.com

ORGANIZATIONS

American Federation of Aviculture
P.O. Box 7312
N. Kansas City, MO 64116
Phone: (816) 421-BIRD (2473)
Fax: (816) 421-3214
E-mail: afaoffice@aol.com
Website: www.AFAbirds.org

Association of Avian Veterinarians
P.O. Box 811720
Boca Raton, FL 33481
Phone: (561) 393-8901
Fax: (561) 393-8902
E-mail: AAVCTRLOFC@aol.com
Website: www.aav.org

Avicultural Society of America
P.O. Box 5516
Riverside, CA 92517
Website: www.asabirds.org

Canadian Dove Association
P.O. Box 135
Plattsville, Ontario, Canada N0J 1S0
Website: www.canadiandoveassociation.com

International Dove Society
3013 Tarpey Ave.
Texas City, TX 77590
E-mail: IDS8381@aol.com
Website: www.internationaldovesociety.com

INTERNET RESOURCES

American Dove Association
www.doveline.com

Avian Network
www.aviannetwork.com

Avian Rescue Online
www.avianrescue.org

Avian Web
www.avianweb.com

The Aviary
www.theaviary.com

Dovepage.com
www.dovepage.com

Exotic Pet Vet.Net
www.exoticpetvet.net/avian/index.html

Hot Spot for Birds
MultiScope, Inc.
1135 N. Poinsettia Drive
Los Angeles, CA 90046
Phone: (888) 246-8776
Fax: (323) 927-1770
E-mail: email@hotspot4birds.com
www.multiscope.com/hotspot

Raising Pet Doves
www.petdoves.com

RESCUE AND ADOPTION ORGANIZATIONS

The American Society for the Prevention of Cruelty to Animals
424 East 92nd Street
New York, NY 10128-6804
(212) 876-7700
www.aspca.org
E-mail: information@aspca.org

The Humane Society of the United States (HSUS)
2100 L Street, NW
Washington, DC 20037
(202)- 452-1100
www.hsus.org

EMERGENCY SERVICES

Animal Poison Hotline
(888) 232-8870
www.animalpoisonhotline.com

ASPCA Animal Poison Control Center
(888) 426-4435
www.aspca.org

Index

Photo Credits

Eric Ilasenko: 1, 9, 19, 33
John Fowler: 3, 7, 8, 15, 17, 36, 49, 55
Elizabeth May: 6, 60
Gregory Sweet: 4, 5, 13, 16, 21, 22, 23, 25, 28-
    32, 34, 35, 38, 39, 42, 45, 48, 51

Kathy McPherson: 14, 43, 58, 59
Mary Ellen Robinson: 12, 41, 44, 47
Ron Caruso: 24, 26, 46